The Uniforms of the British Yeom

The Westmorland and Cumbe

1819-1856

The following notice appeared in the *Carlisle Journal* on 9 October 1819: 'It is intended to form a corps of Yeomanry in Penrith, and we hope that every man who approves of the gallant conduct of the Manchester Yeomanry [a reference to the 'Peterloo' incident on 16 August] will embrace the opportunity of enrolling his name with these doughty and victorious heroes'.

The Regiment was thus formed in October 1819, the commissions of the first officers being dated October 22nd.

The officer commanding at the outset was the Hon. Henry Cecil Lowther, 1790-1867, the second son of William, 1st Earl of Lonsdale. He had served in the 7th Light Dragoons from 1807, was eventually promoted Lt.-Colonel in the 12th Foot in 1817 and went on half-pay in 1818, having served in the Peninsula and duly received the Military General Service Medal.

The unit was originally called the Westmorland Yeomanry although it had troops both in that county and in Cumberland. The title was changed to the Westmorland and Cumberland Yeomanry in 1843.

In the Lowther Castle estate records is one entry regarding the Yeomanry: 1821, October 24th — Paid Joseph Richardson for entertaining the Westmorland Yeomanry Cavalry on the 10th November, 1819, the time of their swearing in, stamp 1s. — £21 1s 8d.

There were six Troops raised:

Location	*Captain*
Milnthorp, Cumberland	George Wilson (formerly Smyth) of Dallam Tower
Kendal, Westmorland	Edward Wilson of Abbott Lodge
Shap, Westmorland (later at Lowther)	John Henderson of Shap
Dalemain, Cumberland	James Parkin of Shirsgill Park
Edenhall, Cumberland	Sir Philip Musgrave, 8th Bart., of Edenhall
Appleby, Westmorland	Matthew Atkinson of Temple Sowerby

At the raising of the Regiment, Colonel Lowther had brought in as Adjutant Samuel Bromley, formerly a Captain in the 10th Light Dragoons where he had also been Adjutant, and with whom Lowther had served in that Regiment during 1814-1817. Colonel Lowther a … other first-class … egiment was E… (1796-1872), who succeeded Lowther as officer commanding on 30 May 1830.

Contemporary reports state that 'when the Regiment was formed the men wore Skiddaw grey trousers and scarlet jackets, with headgear that was wonderful to contemplate — in shape as much like a big frying pan as anything. The trousers were very rough, and some of the men who could afford it bought garments of better quality to wear when on foot, retaining the rough ones for riding'. Headgear 'like a big frying pan' obviously refers to the bell-topped shako, but the exact shade of the 'Skiddaw' grey trousers is uncertain. By the 1860's the uniform of the Regiment was quite magnificent — probably one of the most striking in either Regular or the Yeomanry Cavalry.

Uniform of 1819. The only known surviving example of dress is an Officer's Foul Weather pattern Shako of about 1820 which is in the Yeomanry Museum at Dalemain House. It is grey felt, covered with waterproof black canvas, and slightly bell-topped. It has a black patent-leather peak, lion's head rings at the top for the silver lines and similar ornaments being provided below for the silver-plated chin chain, which is lined with black leather; the black horsehair plume is held by a black boss, and the shako is 9¾″ in diameter across the top. A corresponding Full Dress Shako would no doubt have been in service, the lace probably being silver for Officers and white for the Men. It would be unwise to speculate about the ornaments and fittings but the plume was possibly black as worn later. Other Ranks would have had the Full Dress Shako only, wearing oilskin covers during inclement weather.

In 1912, R. Scott of the *Observer* office in Penrith published an *Historical Sketch of the Regiment* which had appeared in the *Penrith Observer* in April and May of that year. In this reference was made to an Order Book 'now in the possession of a resident in Penrith'. The entries extended from May 1821 to May 1838, and in three other Books (found later) the record is carried to May 1894. The earliest book is inscribed 'Sir P. Musgrave's Troop of Yeomanry Cavalry, Appleby, May 26th, 1821'. The training in 1821 was at Appleby, and an order issued on May

---

The Front cover by *R. J. Marrion depicts:*
Officer in Parade Dress 1905-1914; Officer Field Service Dress,* c. *1912; Kettle Drummer in Review Order 1887; Troop-Sergeant-Major Drill Order,* c. *1870; and Private in Field Service Dress,* c. *1903-1908.

The Back cover shows an *Officer in Review Order,* c. *1857-1880.*

28th read: 'The Regiment will assemble in field day order at eight o'clock to-morrow morning; every man and horse to be present on parade. Parade with side arms at four o'clock in the afternoon'.

In 1822 training was at Kendal, and an order for May 11th read 'The Regiment will parade for divine service in full dress, with swords and pouch belts, to-morrow morning at ten o'clock; also in the afternoon on the troop parade without arms'. During these trainings, assembly was at 7.45 in field day order, with 'swords, pouch belts, and dress caps without plumes, and cloaks neatly rolled to the length of 22 inches'.

Penrith was the scene of the training in 1823. Pistols formed part of the equipment, and the order to parade 'with side arms, pouches and pistols slung' appears regularly. At the Kendal training in May 1824, Colonel Lowther when ordering an assembly at 7.30 in the morning, added 'in case it should be a wet morning the regiment will hold themselves in readiness to turn out at the sound of the trumpet; and parade at a quarter before four o'clock in the afternoon with swords, pouches, belts and pistols slung on the swivels'.

In May 1825 at Penrith new uniforms were served out. Emphasis was laid on the fact that at the church parade the men were to appear with 'swords, pouch belts and new clothes'. During normal parades they were to be in 'their old jackets and overalls, with caps covered without plumes'; and the troop officers were to impress on their men that 'they were not on any account to part with their old regimentals'. Another dress order was: 'Marching order — Jackets buttoned, caps covered, and sashes; review order — dress jackets and sashes with plumes. Officers in the evenings are to appear with jackets open, dress waistcoats and sashes, and if dining out or attending balls, with swords with dress caps uncovered and plumes'.

In 1828 the corps was ordered to be disbanded, but its services without pay were accepted on April 24th. The Milnthorp Troop was disbanded, and for about 11 years the Regiment was without an adjutant. In spite of this, over the years the Yeomanry throughout the Kingdom were called out in aid of the Civil Power, and in this Regiment's case this first occurred at Appleby on 23 March 1829; here the Appleby Troop maintained order at the execution of a lad aged 17 called William Jennings, escorting him from Carlisle Prison to Gallows Hill.

For many years the training was a movable affair, Appleby, Penrith and Kendal sharing. In 1831 the Westmorland Yeomanry Cavalry were again placed on pay, and the training this year was the first the Regiment had in the Autumn with Lieut.-Colonel

Fig. 1: Officer's Full Dress Hussar Jacket, c. 1830, front and rear view. Scarlet, with white collar and cuffs. All lace, braid, cord and buttons silver. The wide lace on the collar, cuffs, jacket edges and in the back seams is the Orris pattern illustrated in the Tailor's Book for the period 1843-48, see Fig. 6. Scarlet tracing braid on the collar and cuffs has not yet been introduced. Note the wavy tracing braid on the collar and the loops forming a chain down the left edge of the jacket.

Hasell in command. It had been the custom for years to make a rendezvous outside the town fixed for training and march into quarters with a certain amount of state. The Regiment assembled at Crackenthorpe at 3 p.m. on the Saturday afternoon, and next morning mustered in Bridge Street for church service 'in full dress with side arms, caps uncased and with plumes'. Daily orders were for a morning parade in old jackets at 8.30 opposite the Court House, and later an afternoon parade. At the end of the training the Regiment assembled in Marching order to return to their homes.

A lace maker's pattern book shows details under the date of October 1831: Hussar pattern jacket, scarlet, with large Hussar pattern square cord. Overall stripes in Full Dress 2¼″ silver oak lace, in Undress ½″ plain silver lace.

In the next few years the trainings each year were at Crooklands near Clifton in May 1832, at Kendal in May 1833, and in 1834 to 1836 at Penrith, during May, October and October respectively. For the 1836 training the n.c.o's. and privates were ordered to appear 'in dress laced jackets with caps cased and without plumes, cloaks to be in front of the saddles and the valises behind them'.

The late Godfrey Brennan saw and made sketches of an officer's Full Dress shako of the period 1835-1840 at the military tailors, Messrs Hamburger, Rogers & Co., and examples of the first known garments which have survived are shown in Figs. 1-5.

Fig. 2: Other Rank's Full Dress Hussar Jacket, c. 1830. Scarlet, with white collar and cuffs, all braid flat white. Traces of fine silver thread through the braid would suggest a mock silver lace. This garment may have belonged to a Troop Quartermaster.

Fig. 3: Officer's Full Dress Sabretache, c. 1845-50. Red leather pocket with scarlet cloth face, edged with silver Granby lace, the monogram 'W.C.Y.C.' in silver embroidery surmounted by a gold crown with crimson cushions. By about 1856 the lace edging was described as being silver herringbone with centre silver vellum stripe. On the re-introduction of this item in 1897, a scarlet silk centre stripe was substituted. Note the long-tailed 'Y' in the monogram.

Fig. 5: Private's Full Dress Jacket, c. 1845. Scarlet, with white collar and cuffs; all loops and lace in flat white braid except the twisted silver shoulder cords. Both this garment and that in Fig. 2 fasten by means of concealed hooks and eyes down the front edges of the garments.

Fig. 4: Officer's Full Dress Shako, c. 1835-50. (From a rough sketch by the late Godfrey Brennan.) Bell-topped, of black felt with a black feather plume. Silver lace band round top, black leather front peak edged silver, turned-up rear peak edged all round top and bottom in silver. The lines, festoon, cockade and loop are also silver. The centre ornament is a garter badge and crown all in gilt on a silver star. There is a 'V.R.' cypher within the belt, surrounded by the title 'Westmoreland and Cumberland Yeomanry', dating this example as post 1843. As far as is known, no example of a later pattern shako has come to light. It is thought likely that there was a direct change to the Hussar busby in about 1854-55.

N.B. The spelling 'Westmoreland' rather than the more usual 'Westmorland' was used by some writers and appears in the Army List as late as 1907. However, despite the example above, the Regiment itself generally favoured the latter spelling without the second 'e'.

The Regiment paraded on 28 June 1838 in honour of the Coronation of Queen Victoria in full dress with caps uncased, (with plumes), and with valises behind and cloaks in front of the saddles. There were five Troops on parade, each as follows: the Appleby Troop at Appleby, the Kendal Troop at Kendal, and the Dalemain, Edenhall and Lowther Troops all at Penrith.

In 1839 the training took place at Penrith from May 7th, but after six days, due to their satisfactory state of training they were dismissed — soon however to be recalled in aid of the Civil Power, firstly at Penrith on 25 May, and then at Carlisle on August 14th. This was at the time of Chartists unrest, and the Yeomanry stood down on the arrival of two Troops of the 7th Dragoons.

The annual training in 1840 was at Penrith, in 1841 at Kendal, and in 1842 at Appleby. In the latter year the Regiment was again called out in aid of the Civil Power at Carlisle on 22 August. These disturbances lasted about a week and the Yeomanry acquitted themselves with much credit in the face of being abused and stoned by the Chartist mob. Four years later the Regiment was again called out in Penrith and Kendall to intervene between Irish and English labourers who were engaged in the construction of the Lancaster and Carlisle Railway.

Early in 1843, during February and March, the title was changed to the Westmorland and Cumberland Regiment of Yeomanry Cavalry. The uniform was gradually standardised throughout the Regiment, and in its final form was the one described for 1847 below.

After the Regiment had been called out in 1839, a new Troop had been raised at Wigton in 1840; this was later called the Carlisle Troop, and Penrith became the Headquarters of the Regiment. William Franklin, formerly of the 23rd and 19th Lancers and the 7th Hussars, was appointed Adjutant on 25 March 1843.

There are some fine coloured diagrams in a tailor's pattern book of about this date (1843) in the National Army Museum. Both Full and Undress are represented, and the Full Dress Hussar jacket is shown in detail (Fig. 6), and, apart from minor points in the braiding and the usual changes in cut over the years, the basic pattern remained unchanged as late as 1914.

In 1847, new clothing was issued. The order was given for the officers to appear in feathered plumes, and the men in their gauntlet gloves, sabretaches and new white-striped trousers. The men were to have their carbines well cleaned and appointments properly put on.

A print from a painting by R. Harrington of about 1847 (Fig. 7) which was dedicated to Colonel Hasell, shows the *Other Ranks* uniform to be a black slightly bell-topped *shako* with a gold Garter badge on a silver pinwheel; there was white metal binding to the peak and white lace edging to the rear peak which was worn turned up; a white plaited cord was across the front, a white lace band round the top edge and white cap

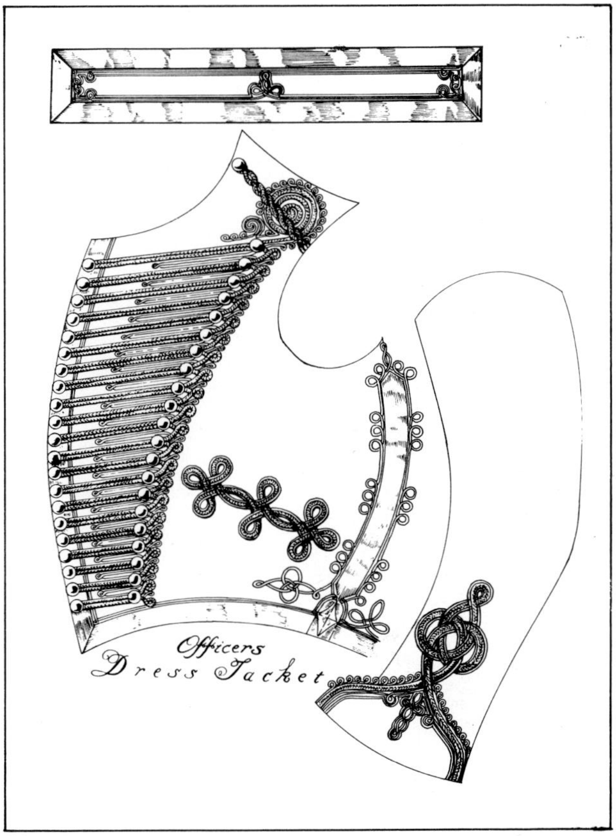

Fig. 6: Officer's Full Dress Jacket, c. 1843-48. Line drawing from a coloured diagram in a tailor's pattern book at the National Army Museum. Scarlet, with white collar and cuffs, the scarlet tracing on the collar and cuffs appearing for the first time. Lace, braid, cord and buttons silver. Apart from slight changes in cut and braiding, the basic design remained in use up to 1914. Note that the overalls are recorded as blue with double silver stripes (not yet on scarlet backing) for Full Dress and with single silver lace for Undress. (Compare with Fig. 8, Full Dress Jacket, 1860-80).

Fig. 7: Sergeant's Mounted Review Order, c. 1847. From a lithograph inscribed 'This print of a Cumberland and Westmorland Yeoman Cavalry Soldier is dedicated with permission to Col. Hasell and the Officers of the Regiment by their obedient servant Sergt. Wm. Sewell'. Painted by R. Harrington. On stone by C.H. Fairland.

Fig. 8: Officer's Full Dress Jacket, c. 1860-80. Scarlet, with white collar and cuffs, the scarlet tracing on the collar and cuffs now being apparent. The badges of rank (in this case a Cornet) are borne on the collar, as was usual between 1860 and 1881. Note the hook between the dummies above the hips (back view) for supporting the barrel sash.

Fig. 9: Detail of Rear Corner of Other Rank's Shabraque, c. 1840-c. 1879.

lines; the chin scales were of white metal, as also the lion's head rings and hooks; a gilt plume socket held a black horsehair plume gathered by a white metal ring. The scarlet *jacket* had about 27 rows of white braid across the front with three rows of small ball buttons; the pocket openings had a white braid edging with a trefoil ornament at either end. The *overalls* were blue with a single white stripe, whilst the cross belt, gauntlets, sword and sabretache *slings* were all white. The *sabretache* was plain black with a rounded lower edge. The *horse furniture* consisted of a blue shabraque, the hind pointed corners being decorated in white embroidery with a crown over 'WCYC', each letter having a small white star over a double spray of oak leaves and acorns, below which was a small white star and tiny ball; the shabraque was edged white, with a blue light showing at the edge (Fig. 9). The sheepskin was black, and the bridle of brown leather.

As the Regiment dressed in Hussar style, it is almost certain that the Other Ranks would have worn a barrel sash similar to the Officers; because of the position of the arm in the picture described above, and because gauntlets are worn, it is not possible to be certain if a sash is worn. However a photograph of the R.S.M. in about 1860 definitely shows a sash (Fig. 13), although by about 1870 they were only worn by Officers.

Fig. 11: Group of Officers, c. 1865. Among the officers in this rare photograph are (seated, front row, third from left) Major the Hon. Henry Lowther, later 3rd Earl of Lonsdale, commanding 1871-76; third from right, Lieut.-Col. Edward W. Hasell, commanding 1831-71; on the extreme right, seated, Captain W. Franklin, the Adjutant. Three, or possibly four types of dress can be seen. They are: 1. Review Order, consisting of the busby and full dress; 2. Drill Order, the forage cap and stable jacket hooked up; 3. Morning or Off Duty Dress, consisting of the forage cap, frock coat and waistcoat. All wear trousers (overalls) with double silver stripes, probably with scarlet backing by this date. The possible fourth type of dress, official or otherwise, is worn by the officer standing second from right, back row. He has apparently turned back the collar and front edges of his stable jacket to reveal the heavily-laced waistcoat, with the white shirt and black tie giving the impression of a roll collar mess jacket. Especially interesting are the tall pattern busbies. Colonel Hasell appears to have the letters W.Y.C. only on his sabretache. It is possible that he and other older officers did not trouble to change to the W.C.Y.C. version. The forage caps are of a very old pattern more appropriate to the 1830's and 1840's; even the Adjutant, Captain Franklin, who has a peak to his cap, wears a type in use prior to and during the Crimean War. By the 1870's, both the forage caps and frock coats had been brought up to date, see Fig. 16.

Sleigh's List of 1850 noted the dress as 'Hussars, without the spare jacket on the shoulder, and white silver lace. The dress and undress jackets of scarlet cloth, with white facings on the collar and cuffs; blue cloth trowsers, with white stripes. Horse appointments: the Hussars' saddle and bridle, with black skin and shabraque. The men's the same, but cotton lace on appointments. Full dress, chaco, silver mounted, with black full-dress feather; the men's, with cotton lace, and black horsehair plume'.

1857-1886

In 1857 a change was made in the accoutrements, light cavalry swords of an improved pattern being issued.

Information on uniform becomes more readily available from about 1857 as there are sources in tailors' pattern books, photographs and actual garments. The following notes from some pattern books were originally written with virtually no punctuation, and the descriptions were almost all in abbreviated form; it has therefore been necessary to make some

Fig. 10: Officer's Undress Sabretache, c. 1850-c. 1898. Both the long and short tailed letter 'Y' were used, apparently in no particular order, in the monogram on the appointments over these years.

alterations in order to render them intelligible. The first entry is interesting in that it shows that by this date the shako had been replaced by a Hussar busby.

'Westmorland and Cumberland Yeomanry 1856-1857 — Busby: of seal, cylinder, 8″ deep (fur brushed round); old regln. red bag, plain and full; hook and eye; screw socket; G.s.p. [= German silver plate] chain and heads. Lines: common silver, 6yds. and egg moulds. Plume: red and white hair with 3-leaf G.s.p. socket (Fig. 11). *Forage cap*: as Cheshire Yeomanry, but in addition a 6-point braid figure, top only. *Pouch:* Embroidered scarlet cloth; *silver W.Y.C.* in cypher and proper crown above; 2⅝″ Artillery loops; laced ¾″ scallop Granby lace; pointed flap'.

No surviving example of the pouch with the flap edged as here described is known to us, but only the type as shown in Fig. 15, which is similar to the 7th Hussars. It is possible that the type referred to is of an earlier pattern, as the Granby lace noted matches the lace on the sabretaches of about 1835-1840 (Fig. 3).

'*Dress Pouch Belt*: red morocco leather, 2¼″; silver herringbone lace and silver vellum lace stripe; wire buckle tip and slide; no breast ornaments. *Tache*: Embroidered monogram and crown as pouch on scarlet cloth; red pocket; laced all round with lace as Pouch Belt. *Dress Sword Belt*: on red morocco; 1″ scallop Granby lace for waist and slings; ¾″ for tache slings; all wire furniture and wire oval buckles. *Sash*: Gold 18 barrels and egg moulds (Figs. 11 and 14). *Sword*: Light Dragoon with black bullion knot. *Gauntlets*: White patent leather. *Undress Tache*: Black patent leather with G.s.p. cypher W.Y.C. and crown (Fig. 10). *Sword Belt*: Black patent leather entire G.s.p., lion's head belt furniture. *Pouch*: Black patent leather with ornament as tache but smaller [altered to W.C.Y.C. and crown]; rings and D's. (Fig. 10). [The additional letter '*C*' was added between *c.* 1845-1856.] *Pouch Belt*: Black patent leather; 2″ with wire buckle tip, slide and breast ornament (bodkin prickers)'. — see Back cover.

Colonel Hasell attended his last training in 1871, having commanded the Regiment for 40 years from 1831. He was succeeded as officer commanding by Henry, 3rd Earl of Lonsdale (1818-1876), formerly a Captain in the 1st Life Guards, whose seniority as Lt.-Colonel was dated 11 May 1872 (Fig. 11).

It was in 1871 that many new requirements were introduced by the War Office. Instead of the haphazard methods previously sufficing, each man had to go through six squad drills and three troop drills — the latter mounted — before assembling for permanent duty; while recruits had to put in a dozen drills between one training and the next. No drill was to be accounted a troop drill unless twelve men properly mounted and equipped were present, and to ensure attention in this matter pay was not to be allowed to any man at permanent duty who had not attended the prescribed number of preliminaries.

At the training of 1873, Lord Lonsdale ordered that troopers should cease to wear gauntlets, which had

Fig. 12: Captain J. Spedding in Mounted Review Order, c. 1868. This is a fine study of an officer in Mounted Review Order. Note the long tailed 'Y' on the shabraque and the short version on the sabretache. By about 1880 the plume became taller and pointed and the busby was reduced in size, the lion's head chin chain holders apparently being retained. Further modification took place in 1897 (see text). The black belts and sabretache were replaced in 1897 by new silver-laced items, the gauntlets having been exchanged for wrist gloves in about 1876. Overalls were replaced by pantaloons and knee boots for mounted duty in 1879-80. N.B. No device is visible in the front corners of the shabraque in this photograph.

Fig. 13: R.S.M. Cropper in Review Order, 1860's. The loops and braid are now in square white Hussar cord. Of interest is the barrel sash, which was abolished about 1870 for other ranks (probably earlier below the rank of sergeant). The R.S.M. wears the plain black leather sabretache, sword belt and slings; from 1873 the 'tache was abandoned by the rank and file although being retained by officers, the R.S.M., Troop Quartermasters and drill sergeants. Finally, by about 1895, it was only carried by officers.

formed part of the uniform for many years; in their place each n.c.o. and man was provided with a pair of buckskin gloves. These had to be taken in charge in the troop stores along with the carbines, sheepskins, shabraques and plumes when not required for regimental parades. Sabretaches, too, had declined in popularity, and were ordered to be worn only by officers, quartermasters and drill sergeants.

In 1874 the training was not until September, and the Colonel in his orders stated that 'little notice has been taken of the remarks made by recent inspecting officers, as to the unusually long and badly fitting footstraps worn by many of the men on parade. He therefore now directs that no other straps than those of a strictly regimental pattern — those for double buttons, and short so as to keep the overalls down on the spur — may be worn on any parade in future, and he holds officers commanding troops responsible that this order is fully carried out'.

A further order in July 1875 after the annual training read: 'Some officers having been furnished by tradesmen with silver laced sword and pouch belts, without the knowledge of the Commanding Officer, their use is to be discontinued from this date. Best black belts, with the regimental letters and silver sword knots, are to be used at Court, public balls, and all State occasions,. This order appears to have remained in force until another member of the Lowther family took command. Hugh Cecil, 5th Earl of Lonsdale (1857-1944) introduced new items of dress, including laced belts, in 1897 (Fig. 15). It is just possible that when the command passed to Colonel Richard Burn in 1876, some laced items were brought back for Levee wear only.

Fig. 14: Lieut.-Col. Richard Burn, Commanding Officer 1876-79. Lieut.-Col. Burn is wearing Review Order. The black crepe mourning band on the left arm is in memory of the late C.O., the 3rd Earl of Lonsdale. Note the black patent belts and 'tache, as ordered by the late C.O. for all orders of dress. Although the incongruous gauntlets were abolished for other ranks in 1873, they were apparently retained for a year or so by the officers, as may be seen in the photograph. The lines have not been placed round the neck in the prescribed manner but are simply draped over the left shoulder.

There are tailors' book entries of April 1878 which show that the *Busby* was 'felt, shape as Artillery and Hussars; Lynx fur; plain scarlet cloth bag; plated 1/8″ chain, and lined black velvet [in 1899 a corded chain on black morocco]; circle 3 [three times round the cap

Fig. 16: Capt. the Hon. St. George Henry Lowther in Undress, c. 1877. The open necked frock coat shown in Fig. 11 has now been replaced by a more modern pattern with stand collar and a new forage cap has been introduced. The overalls are booted, that is re-inforced with leather inside the legs and round the bottoms. These items were never very popular in the Yeomanry Cavalry and many regiments did not wear them; there are, however, other examples of them in use in this regiment. They were replaced by pantaloons and knee boots for mounted duties in about 1879-80.

Fig. 15: Officer's Full Dress Pouches and Belt, c. 1897-1914.

Fig. 17: Front and Rear Views of Field Officer's Full Dress Jacket, 1881-1914. Scarlet, white collar and cuffs with scarlet tracing. Silver wave lace, silver cord and braid. This item was reserved for Levee Dress and special ceremonial occasions after 1905-6.

and later 4 lines circled once] basket cord [particular type of cord], loop for same plated ¾″ with eye, screw socket. The *Plume* of white Osprey, 14″ long, red feathers at base (for the Adjutant, special), or white hair, pointed, with red feathers at base; plated ring and socket. The *Lines* of silver 3 [changed later to 4 × 4] basket cord with swivel (Figs. 11 and 14). The *Cap* (Fig. 20) was the new regulation Forage cap, blue, yeomanry pattern, 2⅜″ deep; a blue welt, and silver embroidered drooping peak; figured on top with two-pennyweight silver braid; 1¾″ silver oak lace band'.

Fig. 18: Other Rank's full Dress Jacket 1880-1914. Scarlet, with white collar and cuffs and white square cord loops and knots. The S.S.M. has silver lace chevrons on scarlet backing and a gold and crimson crown with silver outline.

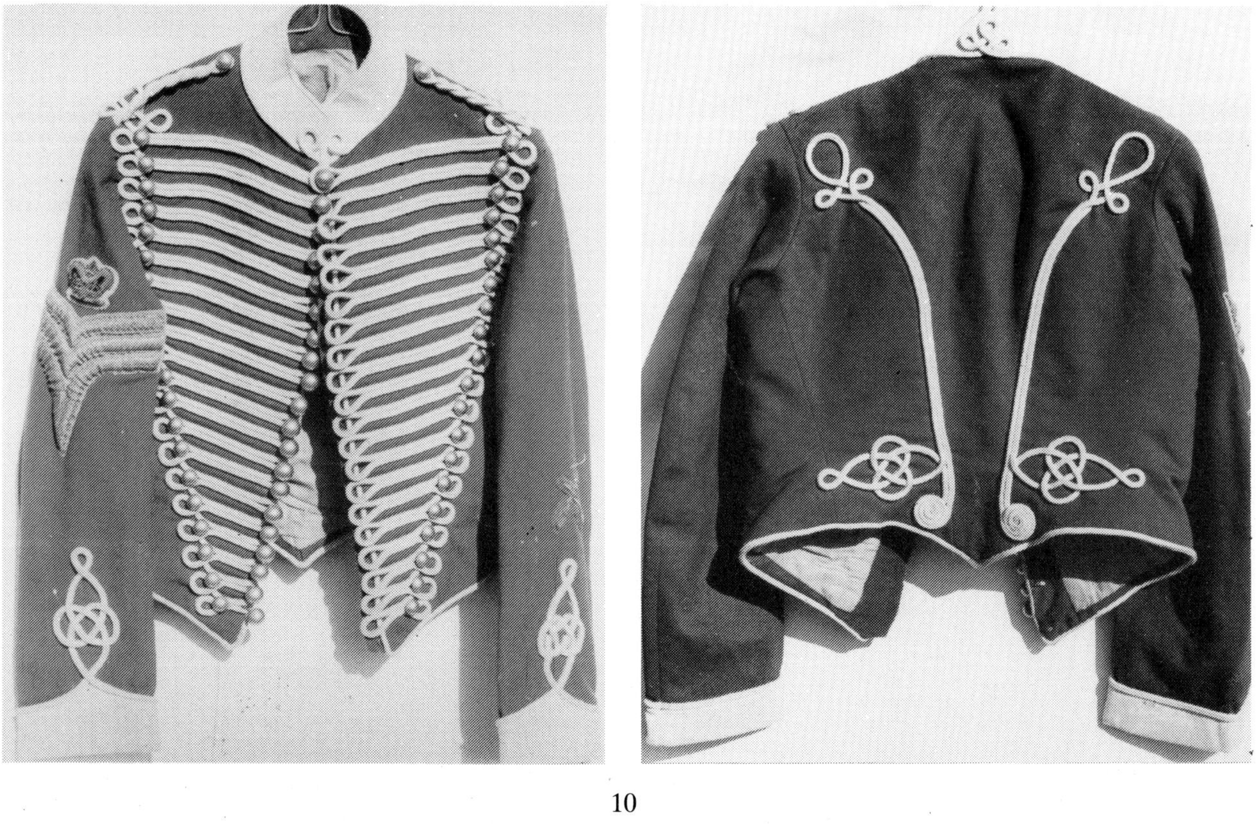

Fig. 19: Group of Officers and N.C.O.s at Dalemain, c. 1888. The group wears Undress; the officer seated left wears a frock coat and the pill box forage cap, while the other seated officer has the 1878 drooping peak pattern cap (apparently worn concurrently), worn with a braided patrol jacket. Both wear overalls with double silver stripes. Most of the N.C.O.s wear 'dismounted drill order', consisting of forage cap, stable jacket, overalls and white pouch belt. Three senior N.C.O.s (1st and 2nd right and centre) have the blue patrol coat, a simplified version of the officer's patrol jacket. Note the wide lace on the forage caps and stable jackets of the Troop Quarter Masters and senior sergeants.

Further entries for August 1878 show the '*Pouch*, black patent leather as Rifle Brigade, round flap; universal tin and plated stud; plated ring loops and plated ornament of W.C.Y.C. and crown (but for morning wear, less ornament). (Fig. 10). *Pouch Belt* of black patent leather, 2⅛"; plated wire buckle tip and slide, breast ornaments plated rose, lozenge and bodkins; 2 plated studs (less breast ornaments for morning wear). The *Sword Belt* of black patent leather, 1" waist, and ¾" tache slings; plated lion's head front and side; rough head buckles (for morning wear, same belt but with snake fastening and wire buckles). The *Tache*, again of black patent leather, regulation, plated W.C.Y.C. and crown (less ornament for morning wear)'. (Fig. 10).

In 1879-1880, pantaloons and knee boots replaced overalls for mounted duties; and in 1881 the badges of rank for officers were removed from the collars and placed on the shoulders (Fig. 20).

1887-1903

We now deal with the uniform of 1887, with changes up to 1903. This is divided between officers and other ranks, in each case into Full Dress and Undress.

OFFICER'S FULL DRESS. (Figs. 17 and 20). Hussar *Busby* of lynx skin, shape as regular 1856 pattern but with a plain scarlet bag and no front boss; plume tapered white horsehair with scarlet vulture feather base, silver-plated three-leaf socket. The *Cap Lines* of three rows of silver basket cord round the cap, body lines worn looped on left breast as R.H.A.; egg mould finials, and plated silver chin chain lined with black velvet. Hussar *Jacket* scarlet with white collar and cuffs, edged all round the jacket and collar with ¾" silver wave lace; Austrian knot on sleeves in silver cord, a chevron on ¾" wave lace below the knots and a small figuring in silver and scarlet braid below the lace on both collar and cuffs (Fig. 17). Plaited silver shoulder cords bearing badges of rank. In front, approximately 23 loops (depending on the height of the wearer) of large silver Russia braid with a fine tracing of half loops between the rows. Three rows of silver buttons down the front, the centre row of ball buttons, the outer rows ½-ball. Side pocket slits with crow's feet and double tracing of silver Russia braid. The back ornamented with two rows of ¾" silver wave lace, a dummy at the bottom of each row over the hips. Tracing braid, forming sets of eyes, down the rows of back seam lace. The distinctions on the sleeves were, for Field officers figuring of regim-

Fig. 20: Group of Officers, c. 1893. Both patterns of forage cap are worn in this group. The majority wear frock coats except the officer standing extreme right, who wears a patrol jacket and no front ornaments (as prescribed for morning wear) on his pouch belt; the officer standing fourth from left, back row, who is in Drill Order (forage cap, stable jacket hooked up and pouch belt); the officer seated far right wears Mess Dress (stable jacket open with waistcoat, shirt and tie); the officer far left, standing, is in Mounted Review Order. Major Hugh Cecil, 5th Earl of Lonsdale, is seated second from left. He commanded the regiment 1897-1908 and introduced many new items of dress.

Fig. 21: Other Rank's Dismounted Review Order, 1897-1905. This fine studio portrait shows clearly the Full Dress in the later years. The busby is of the contemporary 1887 pattern and has both front boss and braided bag. Contrary to other photographic evidence of this date, the subject wears his caplines looped to the left; it is felt that this was the wearer's choice for this occasion rather than prescribed by regulations.

Fig. 22: Officer's Scarlet Serge Patrol or Frock, 1897-1914. From about 1912 the new garments still had the white gorget patches, but double white shoulder cords replaced the shoulder chains and the silver braid on the collar and cuffs was abandoned; plain round silver buttons replaced the lozenge type. Both old and new patterns were worn till 1914.

ental design round the knots, the captains eyes only round the knots, and lieutenants eyes only above the lower part of the knots.

The *Overalls* were dark blue with double silver lace stripes mounted on scarlet cloth, showing scarlet edges and a blue light between the stripes. *Wellington Boots* in dismounted duty with box spurs. *Pantaloons* in mounted duty of dark blue, with stripes as the overalls. The *Knee Boots* black with a 'V' cut in front, spurs with foot chains. *Pouch Belt* and *Pouch, Sabretache* and *Slings, Sword Belt* and *Slings* all in black patent leather (Fig. 10). The *Barrel Sash* of crimson silk cords and gold barrels, acorns and runners. *Gloves* white wrist. *Sword* Light Cavalry pattern with silver knot. *Cavalry cloak* and *cape* of dark blue, lined scarlet, cloak collar blue both sides, long back belt, with silver plated buttons.

The *Horse Furniture* consisted of a *Saddle Rug*, either a leopard-skin with a silver fringe, or a 'Dress' rug of black lamb-skin with scarlet edging. *Shabraque* dark blue, with pointed front and rear corners, edged all round with broad silver lace, mounted on scarlet cloth and showing a scarlet light both sides; on the rear corners was placed the monogram W.C.Y.C. in

Fig. 23: on left, Other Rank's Mounted Drill Order, 1897-1903.

Fig. 24: below, Other Rank's Mounted Review Order, 1897-c. 1905.

silver surmounted by a gold crown with crimson cushions, and, in addition, below the monogram, a double spray of acorns and oak leaves in coloured silks, and a small four-pointed star and tiny ball below the spray (Fig. 12). In the front corners the crown and monogram only was used. The throat plume of black horsehair. *Bridle* of brown leather, with Hussar cross headpiece. Steel head chains until about 1896, and cotton head ropes thereafter.

Changes that took place: prior to about 1890, most known examples of *busbies* were of brown fur; thereafter they were black. In 1897, three rows of silver tracing braid with a button were added to the busby bag, and a silver beehive boss was placed in front (Fig. 25). The overall shape was the regular 1887 pattern. In addition, by 1897, cap lines encircled the busby four times, and, from the same year, the cap lines were looped to the right breast and plaited section from the throat to the point of looping (as worn in the 11th Hussars) was introduced. The chin chain was changed to a corded type on black morocco leather in 1899. Examples of officers' *Full Dress jackets* are known which differ slightly in the braiding, the main difference being in the sleeve ornamentation, which is probably due to the use of tailors other than those officially appointed. Several Field Officers' jackets have been seen which do not have the generally used half-loops of tracing braid in front; these have the tracing extended right across the jacket, completely covering the front of the jacket with silver (Fig. 17).

When the 5th Earl of Lonsdale assumed command in March 1897, he reintroduced Full Dress silver laced *belts and other accoutrements*. These consisted of a pouch belt of red leather mounted with 2″ silver train lace and a centre scarlet silk stripe; the buckle tip and slide were of foliated pattern with a 'VR' in red at the tip in silver wire, front ornaments of silver chains and pickers (Fig. 15). (Examples with plain slide, buckle and tip are known). The pouch was faced with scarlet cloth, which was embroidered with regimental pattern in silver round the edge of the flap; in the centre was the monogram 'W.C.Y.C.' entwined in silver wire, surmounted by a Queen's crown in gold and crimson with a green orb.

In about 1902 a *pouch* with solid silver flap and red leather box was introduced (Fig. 15); it had oak leaf engraving on the flap and the same device as the cloth-faced pouch, but with the King's crown all in gilt, entwined and reversed. This pouch was probably introduced for general wear, such as church parades in order to save the embroidered type for Levees.

The other silver-laced accoutrement introduced in 1897 was a *sabretache* of red leather faced with scarlet cloth, edged all round with silver train lace which had a scarlet silk centre stripe, the device on the face being the same as that on the earlier pouch (Fig. 3). The sabretache slings, sword belt and sword slings were all of red leather with silver lace and centre scarlet stripe.

Lord Lonsdale brought into use a scarlet *pelisse*; this followed closely the Full Dress jacket pattern of lace and braiding. It was trimmed with black fur on

Fig. 25: Honorary Lieut.-Col. F. Markham in Review Order, c. 1901. Colonel Markham wears the 1856 pattern busby, but the busby bag has been updated by the addition of silver braid and button and by the introduction of the boss in front. The lion's head chin chain holders are a relic of an even earlier type of busby. Note the Field Officer's figuring round the Austrian knots on the sleeves. It appears that the Colonel has not placed the cap lines round his neck for the photograph and they are not, therefore, looped up correctly. However, the plaited section introduced *c.* 1897 can clearly be seen.

Fig. 26: Other Rank's Field Service Dress 1902-c. 1908. The white collar, trefoil and piping on the breeches can clearly be seen. Note the web shoulder and waist bandoliers.

the collar and cuffs and had heavy silver cords to suspend it from the left shoulder.

Silver bosses were introduced to the fronts of the officers' *knee boot* in 1897. Additionally, black Hessian boots for Levee wear were adopted in about 1902; they had silver braided tops, bosses and artificial wrinkles.

OFFICERS' UNDRESS 1887-1903. This kit comprised either the 1878 pattern drooping peak forage *Cap* of dark blue with 1¾" silver oak-leaf lace band, silver braid figure, top button and leather peak with ⅞" silver edging; or a Hussar pattern blue pill box, with oak-leaf lace band, silver Russia braid piping round the crown seam, silver netted button and top figure. Both types appear to have been worn concurrently in the years 1887-1900 (Fig. 20). The *Stable Jacket* was scarlet, with white collar and cuffs, silver diamond and point 1" lace all round collar and jacket, which was closed by means of concealed hooks and eyes; there was a row of seed studs down the left front edge; a silver chain gimp at the base of the collar and gimp shoulder cords with badges of rank. The cuffs were edged with a chevron of silver lace; two silver buttons above the cuff at the hind seam. Silver dummy at the bottom of the two back seams over the hips. Full dress *Legwear*. Blue *Frock Coats* braided with black mohair were in use, generally for morning wear and off-duty occasions (Figs. 16 and 20). The *Sabretache, Pouch* and all *Belts* and *Slings* were black patent leather as worn in the Full Dress prior to 1897 (Figs. 10, 12 and 20). Orders in 1889 state that 'the obsolete shabraque straps, at present used for fastening the sheepskins, will be abolished, and returned into saddler-sergeant's stores. Loops will be fastened or sewn on the sheepskins, by which they are in future to be attached to the saddles by means of the holster straps in front and crupper behind. Baggage straps will be cut off the saddles and sewn on to the valises'. This was only the beginning of far-reaching changes, involving both accoutrements and clothing, and abolition of the offices of master saddler and master tailor, which had been in existence for considerably over 70 years.

Fig. 27: Officer's Staff Pattern Forage Cap 1905-1914. This striking scarlet cap with white band and piping had a silver braided peak for the field officers. This pattern of badge started to appear in late 1911, but the earlier type, of three silver sprays of heather, was worn by some officers as late as 1914. One or two plain khaki caps appeared prior to the outbreak of the war in 1914, but most officers continued to wear that illustrated for service dress.

On the other hand greater stringency was brought to bear on men who offended by appearing out of uniform during the trainings without leave, and Sir Henry Vane, Bart., (the officer commanding 1879-1891) threatened that offenders should be most severely dealt with. By the 1890's the use by officers of the stable jacket for drill and as working garment had declined. It was replaced at first by a dark blue-black mohair braided patrol jacket (Figs. 19-20); this in turn being replaced by the scarlet serge frock with white

Fig. 28: Group at Camp in Parade Dress, c. 1912. This shows the Parade or substitute Full Dress for both officers and men for the period 1908-1914. The officer (seated, left) wears the 1911 pattern badge on his cap. His frock has gorget patches but there is no braid on the collar and cuffs and shoulder cords have replaced the chains. Round buttons have replaced the lozenge-shaped ones. However, the officer seated next to him has the old pattern cap badge and the 1897 pattern frock.

gorget patches in 1897 (Fig. 22). From about 1898 the stable jacket was reserved for the officers' Mess Dress only; more elaborate braiding was placed on the back of the jacket and field officers had extra figuring similar to the Full Dress sleeves. A scarlet waistcoat, laced silver, was worn (Fig. 20).

OTHER RANKS' FULL DRESS 1887-1903 (Figs. 18, 21 and 24). This consisted of a Hussar pattern *Busby*, but with a plain scarlet bag and no boss in front; the plume of white-over-scarlet horsehair; (from 1897 the busby became the regular 1887 pattern and shape, with white boss in front, white braid and button on the bag); the cap lines of white cord, at first worn short and hanging in front of the throat in the style of the 7th Queen's Own Hussars, and later (about 1885) looped on the left breast as in the R.H.A. and finally (about 1898) the looping was on the right. When the busby was not worn, the loose ends of the lines were brought up under the left arm and secured to a lower left button in front. The Hussar *Jacket* was scarlet with white collar and cuffs, twisted shoulder cords, white loops in front and Austrian knots on the sleeves. The back seams were also ornamented in white cord. There were three rows of silver buttons down the front of the jacket; the centre row was ball-shaped, the outer rows half ball. The n.c.o.'s chevrons were of silver lace on a scarlet ground. *Legwear* consisted of blue pantaloons when mounted or overalls dismounted, both having double white stripes. *Boots* were either black knee with a 'V' cut, spurs and foot chains, or Wellington and box spurs (Figs. 21 and 24). The cavalry *Cloak* was all dark blue; white wrist *Gloves* were worn and the accoutrements were white *Pouch Belt* and *Sword Belt* with slings, a black pouch and sword with a white sword knot.

OTHER RANKS' UNDRESS 1887-1903. A blue pill box forage *Cap* with a white band and button and white Lancer piping in the quarter seams. Sergeants and above had deeper bands to their caps and the button, piping and band were in silver (Fig. 19, and also Front cover 4th figure from left).

The *Stable Jacket* was scarlet and had a white collar and pointed white cuffs; the shoulder cords were white, with a small silver button at the top of each; down the front of the jacket were about 10 similar buttons and there were two above each cuff seam; for sergeants and above there was a narrow silver lace edging the pointed cuffs and the top and front edge of the collar; the quarter-master's and sergeant-major's had, in addition, silver lace edging down the front and bottom edges of the jacket which was closed by the same method as the officers; n.c.o.'s chevrons were as Full Dress, as were the *Legwear, Belts, Pouch*, etc. (Fig. 19).

By 1892 a blue serge Service *Frock* had been introduced for wear at drill and work by the O.R.'s. Standing Orders of 1892 refer to it: 'The following Regulations on wearing the Blue Service Frock are to be most strictly enforced and adhered to by every Officer and member of the Regiment, without exception: 1. Officers will only wear Patrol Coats when members wear the Blue Service Frock, Musketry alone excepted. N.B. — Frock Coats being resumed by them as usual immediately after parades. 2. The blue Service Frock will always (and only) be worn on the following occasions: (a) All Mounted Drills and Parades. N.B. — Except when scarlet is specially notified in Orders. (b) All Squad Drills. (c) All Musketry. (d) Marching in or out (Troop Drills or Permanent Duty). N.B. No excuse whatsoever will be given or taken as to the Frock being out of repair, etc., on the above occasions. 3. The Service Frock will be worn (without exception) by all members up to 1 p.m. daily. N.B. — Sunday and Inspection Day excepted. 4. Scarlet must be worn by all members after 1 p.m. daily. N.B. — Except Troop Sergeant-Majors and Troop Quarter-Masters, who must wear their Patrol Coats. 5. On returning from a Mounted Drill or Parade (after 1 p.m.) all members will immediately resume the scarlet uniform of the Regiment. N.B. Except Troop Sergeant-Majors and Troop Quarter-Masters, who will resume their Patrol Coats (Fig. 19). 6. On marching in for Preliminary Troop Drills or Permanent Duty every member, without exception, will immediately on dismounting change into scarlet. N.B. Except Troop Sergeant-Majors and Troop Quarter-Masters who will change into Patrol Coats. 7. On marching out (if after 1 p.m.) no member will, on any account, put on the Service Frock till actually preparing to mount'. The exact pattern of the 'Blue Service Frock' is, as yet, unknown, but it was probably a simple blue serge without pockets.

An important change was made in 1893 by the dropping for most purposes of the troop designations, and grouping them into squadrons, as follows:

Appleby and Lowther Troops became A Squadron (Major F. Markham)
Dalemain and Kendal — B Squadron (Major J. Fitzroy Bagot)
Carlisle and Edenhall — C Squadron (Captain G.G. Kirklinton)

In March 1896, the Whitehaven Troop was enrolled, and that at Kendal disbanded, and at the same time the following changes took place:

Appelby and Lowther became A, with H.Q. at Appleby
Edenhall and Dalemain became B, with H.Q. at Penrith
Carlisle and Whitehaven became C, with H.Q. at Whitehaven.

Later this was changed to four Squadrons:

A with H.Q. at Kendal — C—H.Q. at Whitehaven
B—H.Q. at Penrith — D—H.Q. at Carlisle.

The *swords* of other ranks were now carried on the saddle instead of from slings on the body (Figs. 23-24). White cotton head ropes replaced the former steel chains in the horse kit for all ranks about 1896. The exact date of the abolition of the *shabraque* for O.R's has not been established, but it was probably about 1879-1885.

When the 5th Earl of Lonsdale (Fig. 20) assumed command in 1897, he introduced a number of new items: the scarlet pelisse already mentioned, a scarlet serge undress frock for all ranks (Fig. 23); also red, yellow and white braid and lines for the band, and new Full Dress laced belts, sabretache and pouch for the officers. At about the same time, the forage caps of the O.R's lost the Lancer piping and became similar to the officers and ornamented with a Hussar figure on top.

For drill and work, the officers' Undress consisted of either the drooping peak type forage *cap* or the pill box; the new serge *frock* (Fig. 22) was entirely scarlet except that there was a trefoil in mixed silver and red cord on the cuffs and similar cord all round the collar forming eyes below the top edging. On the collar were white gorget patches with a central horizontal red stripe and a lozenge-shaped button near the pointed ends of the patch. There were shoulder chains on scarlet backing and a scarlet waist band or self-belt secured in front by the lowest button. The frock had patch and pleated breast pockets and patch pockets below the waist; five silver lozenge-shaped buttons down the front, a smaller lozenge button on each breast pocket flap and one on each shoulder chain. All the buttons were engraved 'WCYC' and surmounted by a crown (Fig. 22). Full Dress *legwear* and *belts*, together with tan wrist *gloves*, completed the kit. Other Ranks had a similar scarlet *frock* but made of a heavy baize (Fig. 23). It was complete with pockets and self-belt, and had lozenge-shaped buttons similar to the officers. The shoulder chains were on scarlet serge pads; on the collar were gorget patches with a red stripe and button. The trefoils on the cuffs were in ¼″ white Russia braid; the *headgear* was the new pattern pill box; the *legwear* and *belts* were as in Full Dress, and a blue cavalry *cloak* completed their dress.

Immediately after the Penrith training in 1897, a representative contingent went to London for the Diamond Jubilee celebrations, consisting of 4 officers and about 26 O.R's. They all wore the Mounted Review Order, the officers having the new pelisses, silver-laced belts and sabretaches, all with scarlet stripes — but apparently not yet with the front ornaments on the pouch belts. The officers' horse furniture included shabraques, black dress lamb-skins, black throat plumes and cross headpieces. The other ranks did not have saddle rugs, but carried rolled cloaks on the front arch. All ranks were mounted on chestnut horses with white head ropes and up-to-date saddlery. The military artist Harry Payne noted the detachment.

In 1899 during the war in South Africa, men from the Regiment served in the 24th Company, 8th Battalion, Imperial Yeomanry.

Between 1902 and 1903, Khaki clothing was introduced both for field dress and work. The upturned left brim of the *Slouch Hat* bore a spray of artificial heather and a white ribbon rosette. Officers wore a khaki serge *Frock* with a civilian-cut collar that bore a pair of white gorget patches with a red cord down the centre of each, and a small bronze button at the point; a white shirt and collar with a black tie was worn. There were three bronze buttons down the front of the frock, the bottom one holding a khaki self waist belt. There were two patch and pleated breast pockets with buttons and two similar pockets without buttons below the waist. The khaki shoulder straps bore bronze rank badges; the pointed khaki cuffs had a trefoil in white Russia braid. Drab Bedford cord *Breeches* with white piping were worn, and tan leather *Leggings* and ankle boots. A Sam Browne belt and a sword in a leather-covered scabbard completed the kit.

The other ranks (Fig. 26 and Front cover extreme right) also had the *Slouch Hat* (or alternatively the pill box forage *Cap*), and khaki *Frock* similar to that of the officers but with a full white stand collar, a trefoil on the cuffs and the letters 'WCIY' in bronze on the shoulder straps. Riding *Breeches* with white piping down the side seams were worn, khaki puttees and black ankle boots. Both web, shoulder and waist, ammunition bandoliers were worn together for a period.

In about 1905 a very striking staff pattern, peaked, forage *Cap* (Fig. 27) was introduced for the officers. It was scarlet, with a white band and piping in the crown seam, and a black chin-strap held by two silver lozenge-shaped buttons. The black patent leather peak had a silver-braided edge for the field officers. A silver badge of three sprigs of heather was worn. This new forage cap was worn with service dress from about 1905, instead of the slouch hat and also with the scarlet parade dress. By 1905 the old Hussar full dress with busby was reserved for officers attending Levees and special ceremonial occasions — the saving for new young officers must have been considerable. For most 'Dress' parades — and for walking out by the men — the uniform consisted for officers of the new peaked forage *Cap*, the 1897 pattern scarlet serge *Frock, Overalls* with double white stripes on scarlet backing, *Wellingtons* and box spurs, the Full Dress *Pouch Belt*, sword slings and sword with knot (Front cover 1st figure on left). The kit for other ranks was the pill box forage *Cap* worn with the scarlet serge *Frock* of the 1897 pattern (Fig. 23), together with *Overalls, Wellingtons* and spurs.

1908-1914

On the formation of the Territorial Force in 1908, the Regiment became in 1909 part of the Welsh Border Mounted Brigade, and was then stationed as follows:

R.H.Q. — Penrith
A Squadron — Kendal
B Squadron — Penrith
C Squadron — Whitehaven, and a Troop at Barrow
D Squadron — Carlisle

Several changes were made from about 1907. The slouch hat was abolished, and replaced by a plain khaki, peaked, forage cap for the men; from 1908-

Fig. 29: The Wireless Section at Lowther Park Camp, 1914. The other ranks wear plain regular pattern service dress, while the 2nd Lieutenant on the left has obtained a plain khaki forage cap; he still wears the gorget patches on his collar, but his rank insignia is worn on the cuffs in regulation fashion.

1909 the first pattern white-embellished khaki serge frock was gradually replaced by the plain regular cavalry type (Fig. 29); the shoulder titles from about 1909 were T above Y, over W & C on the curve all in brass. Also from about 1910, a leather, 50-round, bandolier was taken into use instead of the former web pattern.

There were other improvements in dress on joining the T.F. Other ranks adopted the officer's pattern scarlet and white peaked forage cap, the badge being embroidered in white worsted on scarlet cloth — an oval within a laurel wreath inscribed Westmorland & Cumberland Y. surmounted by an Imperial crown; and the old full dress scarlet Hussar jackets were once more issued to the men to be worn for camp church parade and special ceremonial events, but with the new forage caps and not the busby (Fig. 28).

A photograph of A Squadron taken at annual camp in 1911 shows an officer in the peaked forage *cap* and the scarlet *serge*; the latter now has ordinary round buttons and the waistband has disappeared, although both the gorget patch and the crowsfoot on the cuff are still there. Blue *overalls* with double white stripes on a scarlet backing are worn, together with the full dress *pouch belt*, sword with dress slings and knot, and brown wrist gloves. This uniform was worn for most dress parades, the men wearing the scarlet and white peaked *caps*, the full dress Hussar *jackets*, and *overalls* and cap lines until 1914 (Fig. 28). On certain occasions other ranks wore the 50-round brown leather ammunition bandoliers with Full Dress.

An extract from Camp Standing Order for 1911 records that 'No dress other than Uniform will be worn in Camp. 2. Men on 'pass', and those walking out beyond the Bounds of Camp, will invariably be dressed in Tunic, Block Front Boots [Wellington] Swan Neck Spurs, Forage Caps and carry a whip or light cane. 3. For Main Guard, men will parade in Drill Order, with Rifles and Bayonets, and Cloak folded 'en banderole'. 4. For Stable Guard, Fatigue Dress, Cloak and Forage Cap. 5. The wearing of civilian caps or coats is strictly prohibited'.

In the above Orders, it should be noted that the tunic referred to is in fact the scarlet serge Frock, and Full Dress overalls completed the walking out order.

In 1911, Major C. Beddington, always anxious to keep his Squadron in the front line of modernity, equipped it at his own expense with a portable radio outfit. The fixed part of the 'contraption' was in a tent near the officers' mess, and the portable parts were carried about on horseback, although later a limbered wagon was used. The apparatus was much in use on local manoeuvres (Fig. 29). In May 1912 Major Beddington decided to publish a wireless newspaper for the benefit of the Regiment. In those days the radio system of communication was in its infancy, and messages were sent and received in Morse code.

The Regiment furnished a dismounted detachment of 1 officer and 25 O.R's. at the Coronation of King George V in June 1911; they formed part of the 2nd Battalion of the Yeomanry Brigade, and with other yeomanry detachments lined the streets at Hyde Park Corner and Piccadilly. There are two photographs showing the Westmorland and Cumberland; the officer wore complete Dismounted Review Order consisting of the busby with lines, a Full Dress jacket, overalls, pelisse, barrel sash, laced pouch belt and sword slings, but not a sabretache. The other ranks wore the scarlet and white peaked forage cap, the Full Dress jacket, cap lines and overalls (Fig. 28); rifles were carried, but the S.S.M. paraded with a sword.

Late in 1911, tailors' notes refer to a new pattern of badge for the officers' scarlet and white peaked cap. This badge was embroidered in silver wire on scarlet cloth, and was in the form of a circlet surmounted by an Imperial crown with crimson cushions, and inscribed Westmorland and Cumberland Yeo., within which were three sprigs of heather (Fig. 27).

By 1914, the officers' service dress had hardly altered from that worn in 1903, except for the cap badge as just noted, and that from about 1913 the new khaki frocks had the regulation rank badges and braiding on the cuffs, dispensing with the trefoil. The riding breeches still had white piping but tan knee boots had for the most part replaced leggings (Fig. 29 and Front cover, 2nd from left).

When mobilised for service in August 1914, the men were ordered to take their dress peaked forage caps, the Full Dress jackets and overalls for walking out wear. These, however, were soon returned to their respective headquarters.

The Regimental Band and Trumpeters, 1852-1914

In the 1852 Regimental Order Books there is the first mention of the Band. On their music pouches, the bandsmen had an oval brass plate on which was engraved 'WCYC', with a crown above the plate.

For Undress in 1854, the band wore an all-blue muffin-shaped forage cap. They wore a special 'band lace' down the front and all round their scarlet stable jackets, as also round the white collar and on the white pointed cuffs; on their trousers a single stripe of the same lace. This lace was mixed red, white and blue, giving a speckled effect. The earliest known photograph of a bandsman — indeed the first photograph of any member of the Regiment — is that of Bandsman R. Taylor (said to have been taken in 1854) in which he wears the Undress uniform described (Fig. 30).

The Band's wide bass drum was first used for the opening of the Appleby and Eden Railway in 1858; this was reported in the contemporary press.

By 1862, a Hussar busby of the same pattern as that worn by the rest of the Regiment, but with an all red plume, was in use by the Band (Front cover, mounted figure). A photograph shows them (Fig. 31) wearing a pill box forage cap with a narrow white band and white piping crossed in Lancer fashion. Double white stripes are now on the trousers.

In about 1865 the blue in the Band lace was abandoned, and the use of the oval plate on bandsmen's pouches was discontinued in 1870. By 1877, the Undress consisted of a scarlet pill box forage cap with a white band, quarter seam Lancer welts and button. The stable jacket was plain scarlet, with a white collar and plain pointed white cuffs; there were about 10 small silver buttons down the front; the front edge only was piped white, and there was white Lancer piping in the back; also a small button above each cuff. The overalls were as in Full Dress.

A photograph of R. Taylor (now the Bandmaster) taken about 1870 is the first known to show the Full Dress of the Band (Fig. 32). Taylor wears the busby with an all-red plume as worn by the Band and trumpeters; his Full Dress jacket is similar to the other ranks, but with red and white speckled cord and cap-lines, white pouch belt and black pouch. His overalls of dark blue have double white stripes; his sword and sabretache slings are white, the sabretache black and the swords knot white. The horse furniture is of a black lamb-skin with white serrated edge, a

Fig. 30: Bandsman R. Taylor, c. 1854 (from a daguerrotype). This is the earliest known photograph of any member of the Regiment. No doubt the forage cap which Bandsman Taylor wears is the other ranks version corresponding to that worn by the officers in Fig. 11.

Fig. 31: The Bandsmen, c. 1862. Note the cap case on the pouch belt near the right arm of the figure on the left and the double white stripes on the overalls.

band shabraque similar to the mens' but in red, bearing the monogram in white letters having crimson centres and four small white stars superimposed and inset in the monogram, over a double spray of white oak leaves with crimson acorns, a white star with crimson centre beneath and a white ball below the bottom point of the star; the whole is surmounted by a gold crown with green orb and gold bar, white jewels round hoops, and crimson cushions. The jewels on the band of the crown are red, green, red, green, below which white ermine with black ticks. The shabraque was edged round with broad white lace. A steel head chain and red throat plume are worn.

A photograph probably taken at Penrith during Queen Victoria's Golden Jubilee in 1887, shows the Bandmaster and kettle drummer mounted. Drum banners are being carried (Front cover, mounted figure) and the mounted men both have shabraques and sheep-skins, but only the Bandmaster has kneeboots; the kettle drummer wears overalls, as apparently do the others just visible. The remainder of the uniform is as described for Bandmaster Taylor in 1870, except that he now wears pantaloons, and the bandsmen (except the Bandmaster and kettle drummer) appear to have sheep-skins only and no shabraques. It is not possible to be certain of the colour of the drum banners, but from the tone in the photograph it would not be unreasonable to assume they were probably red. There is a broad band of light (possibly white) lace at the top and bottom of the banners, with a row of (possibly white) points or teeth pointing downwards, round and below the top lace, the same pointing upwards above the bottom lace. The centre device is exactly as that described for the shabraque but a little larger. Steel head chains complete the horse kit (not visible in the drawing). The Bandmaster rides a cream or grey horse, while the kettle drums are mounted on a dark animal with a light mane and tail. The drummer has a white throat plume, the Bandmaster none; see also Fig. 33 of the Band in about 1883.

Fig. 32: Bandmaster R. Taylor, c. 1870 in Mounted Review Order. Note the shabraque and the long-tailed 'Y' in the monogram. The belts and slings are white, the sabretache without ornament and the barrel sash is not worn.

In 1897 Lord Lonsdale introduced yellow (his family colour) to the Band lace making a red, white and yellow speckled mixture. This, however, had a fairly short life, for when the Full Dress jackets were reintroduced in 1908, the Band were issued with jackets which had plain white cord and white lines as worn by the O.R's of the Regiment. They also adopted the new peaked scarlet and white forage cap in place of the busby (Fig. 35), except for the kettledrummer who, when mounted, continued to wear the old pill box cap (Fig. 36).

The uniform of the trumpeters was the same as that of the bandsmen. It appears that prior to about 1908 the trumpet cords were in the same speckled mixture as the band lines and braid, but from that date the trumpet cords and fringes were plain dark green.

Fig. 33: The Band, c. 1883 (probably at the Two Lions Inn, Penrith). The uniform is the Review Order of the Regiment, with the distinctions of the all-red plume, and the red and white speckled 'Band' lace and lines. Note the very wide bass drum, almost certainly the drum first used at the opening of the Appleby and Eden Railway in 1858. Three members are said to be absent from the photograph.

Fig. 34: Bandsmen and Trumpeter, c. 1896. The forage cap with Lancer quarter piping is still worn, as is the red and white 'Band' lace. Note the arm badge of the standing trumpeter.

Fig. 35: Trumpeter, c. 1908. A very clear study of the Parade Dress of the period 1908-14. This trumpeter wears the uniform worn by all other ranks of the Regiment for dress occasions. Note the all-green trumpet cords and the cap lines, yet again looped to the left (probably at the individual's whim on a private occasion).

Fig. 36: The Kettledrummer, c. 1912. This shows the last man to wear the pill box forage cap. No drum banners are carried and the horse has no throat plumes.

Fig. 37: The End of an Era: Kettledrummer at Lowther Park Camp, 1914. This shows a new drum horse, 'Pompey', and a youthful new drummer at the last camp, immediately before the outbreak of World War 1. The drummer wears plain khaki regulation service dress. Note the Leopardskin and the scarlet throat plume.

A photograph in Lowther Park of about 1901 shows the Bandmaster wearing the officer' pattern drooping peak forage cap, frock coat and overalls; the bandsmen have their pill box caps, Full Dress jackets and lines (all of which are still speckled) and overalls. The occasion was of course informal, otherwise the busbies would have been worn.

POSTSCRIPT

1914-1967

The Regiment served throughout the Great War, and on the re-constitution of the Territorial Army it was converted to the Royal Artillery. Initially in 1922 it became 93rd (Westmorland and Cumberland) Brigade, R.F.A., but in 1923 it was renumbered 51st. It served in the World War as 51st Field Regiment, and in 1947 became 251 (Westmorland and Cumberland) Field Regiment. On further reorganisation of the T.A. in the 1960's, it was reduced to 851 (Westmorland and Cumberland) Independant Field Battery, and in 1967 it formed part of the 4th (Territorial) Battalion, the Border Regiment.

The Westmorland and Cumberland Yeomanry was one of the last regiments to retain a mounted regimental band; indeed, at the last camp before the Great War held at Lowther Park in 1914, the Band paraded in camp mounted (Fig. 37).